Dr Hibernica Finch's Compelling Compendium of Irish Animals

**AGA GRANDOWICZ
ROB MAGUIRE**

Little Island

Introduction from Dr Finch

Pay no mind to what the cat says – curiosity is a *wonderful* thing.

Curiosity has climbed mountains, propelled us into outer space, and even proved that pineapple works splendidly on pizza.

My own curiosity has led me to explore as much of the world of Irish animals as could possibly be done in a polite fashion.

It began in my garden as a child, where I whiled away the hours chatting with slugs and snails and worms. Who were these slimy visitors? Where did they come from? Why did they seem to enjoy eating leaves and earth as much as I enjoyed eating ice-cream?

I had many questions, and spent much of my childhood on a hunt for answers. Each answer was so brilliantly curious, so utterly fascinating, that it threw up another question.

One should never be afraid to ask questions – because you never know what amazing things the answers could lead to.

My journey of discovery went on and on and on, from animal to animal to animal, until eventually my darling parents asked a very important question: 'Hibernica, what would you like to be when you grow up?' There was only one answer in my mind. A dolphin. Unfortunately, that was quite out of the question – so I became a zoologist instead.

Over many years in this line of work I have swum with seals off Cape Clear, camped with corncrakes in Connemara, and picnicked with pine martens in the Phoenix Park. Each experience was even more exciting than the last.

So as you open the pages of this compendium and meet some of this country's most compelling creatures, I hope that it kick-starts a quest that is as fun for you as mine has been for me.

Hibernica Finch.

Air

Land

Water

White-Tailed Bumblebee	1
Common Darter	3
Marsh Fritillary Butterfly	5
Lesser Horseshoe Bat	7
European Robin	9
European Storm Petrel	11
Great Spotted Woodpecker	13
Atlantic Puffin	15
Short-Eared Owl	17
European Herring Gull	19
Eurasian Pygmy Shrew	21
Viviparous Lizard	23
Western European Hedgehog	25
Red Squirrel	27
Irish Hare	29
Eurasian Otter	31
European Badger	33
Red Fox	35
Red Deer	37
Natterjack Toad	39
Purple Sea Urchin	41
Three-Spined Stickleback	43
Common Hermit Crab	45
Atlantic Salmon	47
Common Seal	49
Bottlenose Dolphin	51
Killer Whale	53
Basking Shark	55
Glossary	57

White-Tailed Bumblebee

(Bombus lucorum)

IRISH NAME: Bumbóg earrbhán
CLASS: Insecta

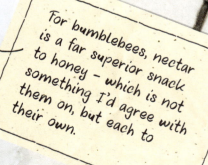

Nectar pots

The white-tailed bumblebee trundles busily through life. Bees are thought of as busy because they buzz about providing one of nature's most important services: delivering pollen from plant to plant. Plants need this to happen so there can be new plants.

It's fortunate that bees are messy eaters. When they visit a flower in search of pollen and nectar to eat, some of the pollen sticks to the bee's body like crumbs getting stuck to a jumper. The polleny bee then buzzes along to another flower, where some of the pollen gets left behind, allowing a new seed to form.

Plants are a central part of a healthy ecosystem. That means they are really important to all the animals on the planet – bees, goats, elephants, crickets, blackbirds, humans, everyone – and bees (all kinds of bees, not just our friendly bumbles) perform the important task of pollination for all our benefit. They are just foraging for food for themselves, of course, and very probably don't realise the important job they're doing for the rest of us.

Bumblebees don't make much honey – that's the job of their cousins, the honey bees. Bumblebees collect nectar and pollen, and they store the nectar in tiny pots for when they're hungry.

Another difference from the honey bee is that bumblebees don't die when they sting. However, there's no need to panic about getting stung at all, since bumblebees are usually far too busy to give you even a second thought.

Several types of bumblebee found in Ireland are now endangered, which is a problem for us all.

For bumblebees, nectar is a far superior snack to honey – which is not something I'd agree with them on, but each to their own.

Essential facts

⟷ **SIZE:** Regular white-tailed bumblebees are roughly 12mm in length, but the queen bee (the mother of the colony) is around 16mm long.

🏠 **HOME:** Bumblebees live together in colonies of anything from thirty to four hundred sisters (and just a few brothers).

🍴 **DIET:** The majority of bees in a colony are workers: female bees who fly (sometimes distances of several kilometres) to gather nectar and pollen, which bumblebees like to eat.

🎂 **LIFE:** Most bumblebees only survive for a few months, but the queen bee lives for roughly a year.

Twenty different species of bumblebee are native to Ireland, and six of these species, rather than starting their own colonies, simply lay their eggs in the colonies of other bumblebees, leaving the workers to raise their young for them.

Common Darter

(Sympetrum striolatum)

IRISH NAME: Sciobaire coiteann
CLASS: Insecta

With its distinctive bright red suit, there are few insects with a sense of style as well formed as that of the common darter dragonfly. But common darters don't just sit around looking pretty. Instead, they use their amazing wings to zoom around catching insects. They can move their wings independently of each other, which means they can change direction or stop dead in the air in the space of a wingbeat.

Dragonflies spend most of their lives in water as nymphs. Once they do get their wings, common darters tend to zip about at a great rate, but they never stray far from the water.

Contrary to what Dubliners might think, the name 'common darter' does not mean these insects frequently take the train. In fact, the name describes how the darter hunts for food – it hovers in the air, patiently waiting, before sharply darting at its prey with lightning speed.

If I had to wait for years and years for wings, I've no doubt that I'd be getting as much use out of them as possible once I finally got them.

A nymph that doesn't have its wings yet

Essential facts

 SIZE: These distinctive dragonflies have wingspans of only around 30mm.

 HOME: Dragonflies spend as much time as possible near water. Think rivers, lakes, and, in particular, bogs.

 DIET: As committed carnivores (meat-eaters), these agile fliers are always on the hunt for smaller insects they can feast on. Their huge eyes mean that they can see very well, which helps them to catch their food. Dragonfly nymphs are the biggest predators of tadpoles in Irish ponds and rivers.

LIFE: Dragonflies can live for up to four years, but only about six months of this is as an actual dragonfly. The vast majority of their life is spent as a nymph – which is a smaller, wingless version of what they'll eventually end up as.

Since Ireland is lucky enough to have plenty of water, we never have to go too far to spot one of these eye-catching creatures. If you have a garden pond, you should see them there from early summer to mid-autumn.

Marsh Fritillary Butterfly

(Euphydryas aurinia)

IRISH NAME: Fritileán réisc
CLASS: Insecta

You might think that a creature as beautiful as the marsh fritillary butterfly would like to live somewhere more elegant than a bog. The gardens of Versailles, perhaps, or the Hollywood hills. However, you won't find the marsh fritillary in places like that, but flittering about the marshes and bogs of Ireland, busying away at the flowers like a host constantly expecting a visitor.

This radiant butterfly is very picky about the place that it calls home. There will have to be a good supply of its favourite plant, the devil's bit, and the land itself should ideally be open and unrestricted. Even a hedgerow has been known to irritate the marsh fritillary – it'll refuse to move beyond the hedge, instead staying put (and possibly sulking).

Sadly, this particular persnicketiness about its habitat has made life a tad more difficult for the marsh fritillary. Partly for this reason, the species is on the decline in Europe. It is doing better in Ireland, which is good news, but it's still quite rare, so count yourself lucky if you spot one.

Like all butterflies, marsh fritillaries start life as eggs, then hatch into hairy caterpillars. The caterpillar eats a lot and then spins itself a chrysalis before turning into something that resembles soup. This rather extreme course of action is what needs to be done in order to build a new and more fabulous body, and become what we know as this brightly patterned butterfly.

> Keep your eyes peeled if you're in boggy areas in the midlands or the west of the country, because those are the best places to spot this rare butterfly.

Larva

Essential facts

 SIZE: The marsh fritillary butterfly is one of our rarest butterflies, and its beautifully patterned wingspan ranges from 42 to 48mm.

HOME: Unsurprisingly, you'll find the marsh fritillary most commonly on marshlands and bogs.

 DIET: The marsh fritillary's favourite food is nectar from a flower called the devil's bit. This bluey-purple flower is often found in the places where the marsh fritillary lives – and is particularly common in the west of Ireland.

 LIFE: From the time they are laid as eggs until the end of their lives as butterflies, marsh fritillaries live for about a year. They only exist in their adult, butterfly state for a couple of weeks.

Pupa

Devil's bit – marsh fritillary's favourite flower

Lesser Horseshoe Bat

(Rhinolophus hipposideros)

IRISH NAME: Crú-ialtóg bheag
CLASS: Mammalia

The poor lesser horseshoe bat has an image problem. For one thing, it has a horseshoe-shaped nose that looks rather ugly to us. On top of that, it happens to be a bat – an animal that people aren't particularly fond of. You might think that this would be awfully depressing for the bat, but image isn't everything.

The lesser horseshoe bat's nose is an excellent reflector of sound. This comes in very handy for locating things in the dark by sound reflection (called 'echolocation') – which is good for bats because they come out mostly at night, when it's dark.

In times gone by the lesser horseshoe bat was known as the 'aristocracy bat'. That's because it has a habit of setting up home in abandoned mansions and castles around the country. It will also happily roost in ordinary old houses and sheds, in the space just under the roof.

In winter this bat often moves underground to hibernate in old mineshafts or caves. It hangs upside down by its feet when hibernating, with its wings wrapped around it.

A good reason to be fond of the lesser horseshoe bat is that it loves to eat midges. A lesser horseshoe bat eats thousands of these very small (and very irritating) bugs a day. This means that there are fewer midges to pepper your legs with bites when you wear a pair of shorts on a camping trip.

I sometimes could do with a spot of echolocation myself to stop me bumping into things. In fact, humans have borrowed the idea of echolocation from bats and dolphins. The human version is called 'sonar'.

Maybe instead of the aristocracy bat they should be called the acro-bat.

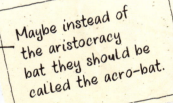

Essential facts

↔ **SIZE:** As the 'lesser' species, this small bat weighs just 5 to 10g when fully grown, but its wings can span up to 25cm.

HOME: These bats live in buildings in the summer and underground spaces in the winter.

DIET: As sleek and elegant fliers, these bats are excellent at hunting all kinds of insects for food, including daddy-long-legs (also known as crane flies), midges and moths. Its hunting grounds are mostly wooded areas, especially near rivers and lakes.

LIFE: The lesser horseshoe bat usually lives about five years, but has been known to live much longer – sometimes up to the age of eighteen.

It's hard to know why people don't like bats, but I expect all the vampire stories don't help. It's lucky that bats can't read.

Lesser horseshoe bats mate in the autumn or the winter, but the females don't get pregnant immediately. Instead, they hold the seed inside their bodies, only releasing it in the spring. That's when the female actually becomes pregnant!

This handy trick means that the babies are only born when the weather is starting to get better and there's plenty of food about.

European Robin

(Erithacus rubecula)

IRISH NAME: Spideog
CLASS: Aves

Most animals seem quite happy with their lot in life, but over the years I've come to suspect that the robin wouldn't mind trying out life as a human. Very few birds are as keen to interact with humans as robins are, and they're particularly eager to set up their nests in human gardens or sheds. I'd like to think this is because they're a very friendly sort, but in reality they have more practical reasons.

Robins are always on the lookout for food. Robins who live in forests have learnt that it's a good idea to follow larger animals, who stomp along unsettling the earth and turning up tasty worms and other treats for the robin to eat.

It's unlikely that robins assume we humans are simply larger, less hairy versions of these forest mammals, but in any case they're not afraid to stick close to us in much the same way.

We know the robin by its nickname 'Robin Redbreast', but not all robins actually have a red breast. Robins moult each year, which means they shed their old feathers and grow new ones. Until their first moult, which is when they grow their bright red bibs, young robins have a rather low-key breast of plain old brown.

The robin is an extremely territorial bird – which means that a robin doesn't like sharing its patch of garden or woodland with other robins. If a cocky bird does take a fancy to its neighbour's territory and tries to move in, things can turn nasty. In fact, it seems that roughly ten per cent of deaths among robins are a result of fighting!

> So what comes across as friendliness is probably just these cute little birds thinking with their tummies. Who could blame them?

> Ireland is positively full of robins – somewhere between three and four million, in fact, nearly as many robins as people.

a young robin

Essential facts

↔ **SIZE:** The robin usually weighs just 20g, and grows to be around 14cm long from beak to tail.

🏠 **HOME:** The robin likes nesting in garden birdhouses with open fronts. You'll also find the robin in woods and forests, or setting up house in trees or walls that are covered in ivy.

🍴 **DIET:** Robins are great fans of worms and insects. However, they also like some fruits. If you want to make a friend of a local robin, leave some apple on your bird table.

🎂 **LIFE:** Robins usually live for one to two years, but some lucky ones survive a lot longer than that. One robin has been recorded as living to the age of nineteen.

European Storm Petrel

(Hydrobates pelagicus)

IRISH NAME: Guairdeall
CLASS: Aves

If there is an animal in Ireland that wouldn't be out of place in a fairytale, it's the storm petrel. There's something magical about these seafaring birds and the places where they make their homes. They live on islands like Skellig Michael – a giant rock that rises dramatically out of the sea off the coast of Kerry.

The storm petrels of Skellig Michael make their homes in tiny holes in the dry-stone walls of the island, and wander out to sea when they feel hungry for fish.

At sea they fly incredibly close to the water, dangling their feet just low enough to skim the surface. This makes it look like the bird has the magical ability to walk on water. It can't, of course, but it's an impressive illusion nonetheless.

The walking-on-water trick is partly where the storm petrel gets its name from. Sailors named the bird 'petrel' after St Peter, who is supposed to have (briefly) walked on water. The 'storm' part came from the fact that petrels were frequently seen by sailors during storms, when the birds would take shelter by hiding in parts of the ship.

Skellig Michael is either one of the most magical places in Ireland or else it's a regular old place that happens to be visiting from a galaxy far far away.

The storm petrel is a big traveller, migrating in winter to the warm southern Atlantic, where it spends the whole season.

Essential facts

⟷ **SIZE:** The smallest seabird breeding in Ireland, the storm petrel only weighs around 27g.

🏠 **HOME:** Large colonies of storm petrels are found on the west coast of Ireland, from County Donegal down to County Cork. The Skellig and Blasket Islands in Kerry are home to some of the biggest colonies. The birds huddle together in nests made in holes in walls, cliffs, rocks or even hidden under vegetation.

🍴 **DIET:** The storm petrel's diet consists of small fish, shellfish, plankton – all manner of small creatures that can be taken from the sea.

🎂 **LIFE:** Storm petrels have been known to survive to the age of thirty.

Great Spotted Woodpecker

(Dendrocopus major)

IRISH NAME: Mórchnagaire breac
CLASS: Aves

If you want to find a woodpecker, your best bet is to keep your ears cocked for their distinctive tapping sound. In fact, there are two kinds of noise made by woodpeckers. Sometimes they're tapping away at the bark of a tree, looking for insects to eat. But at other times they make a faster drumming sound. This is their way of marking out their territory (almost like they're making an obnoxious amount of noise to make sure no one sits beside them).

For many years you would have been as likely to find a unicorn in Ireland as a great spotted woodpecker. There was no shortage of them in Europe, but in Ireland the woodpecker population was considered extinct. What did we do? Had we offended them somehow? It was a mystery.

Then, as the twenty-first century began, an even bigger mystery started to unfold. Year by year the woodpeckers returned. At first we couldn't believe it, but then more came, and more again – every year. Now these mysterious birds are thriving in several areas of Ireland.

There's plenty that's great about this bird, but the name 'great spotted' isn't based on personality or achievement. Here 'great' refers to size. The great spotted woodpecker is quite a large bird, as big as a blackbird. (There is also a lesser spotted woodpecker, but we don't have any of those in Ireland. Yet.)

> Their drumming can be very loud – like nature's version of a construction crew. Which makes me wonder if the woodpecker's neighbours ever get fed up of all the racket.

> The word 'spotted' in this woodpecker's name simply means that it has spots – like the spots on a Dalmatian or a pair of socks. It does not mean 'great spotted' in the sense that someone might say, 'Great! I spotted a woodpecker!'

> The best place in Ireland to find (or hear) a woodpecker is probably Glendalough in County Wicklow.

Essential facts

↔ **SIZE:** When fully grown, a great spotted woodpecker can be as long as 24cm, with a wingspan of 39cm.

🏠 **HOME:** Woodpeckers make small holes in tree trunks to find food, but each year they also set about making one big hole that will become their nest – nice and snug and hidden away from predators.

🍴 **DIET:** Since wood is a great place for insects to hide, it's also a great place for a woodpecker to find some lunch. They also like to visit gardens in suburban areas. Feel free to leave them out some pine cones, in which they find delicious seeds.

🎂 **LIFE:** Great spotted woodpeckers can live for up to eleven years.

Atlantic Puffin

(Fratercula arctica)

IRISH NAME: Puifin
CLASS: Aves

Life can't be easy for the Atlantic puffin. This rather small and delicate bird bears all the hallmarks of cute, and cuteness comes with its own problems. Hordes of admirers, for example. Everyone adores the puffin's delightfully coloured beak and well-coordinated footwear. I suspect that this is why puffins often find themselves living on private islands, like celebrities.

The so-called 'parrot of the sea' doesn't spend the entire year in full colour. In winter the puffin sheds its flashy bill, and instead sports a smaller, duller, greyer beak. Combined with its black and white coat, this makes the puffin in winter almost completely colourless, like the star of an old movie. The reason for this is that the puffin's mating season doesn't begin until spring, so in winter there's simply no point in dressing to impress – no one who matters will be paying attention anyway.

When looking for food the puffin can dive as deep as sixty metres underwater, which is rather impressive. Even more impressive is its not-so-common ability to come back to the surface holding several small fish in its beak at the same time. The puffin has a uniquely shaped beak, with little hooks along the edge which allow it to keep hold of the slippery fish.

If you'd like to see a puffin, the good news is that many of the best places to find them are fantastic places to visit anyway. From Skellig Michael to the Cliffs of Moher, puffins tend to pick places to live that humans find pretty.

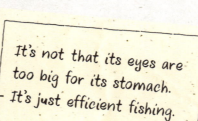

It's not that its eyes are too big for its stomach. It's just efficient fishing.

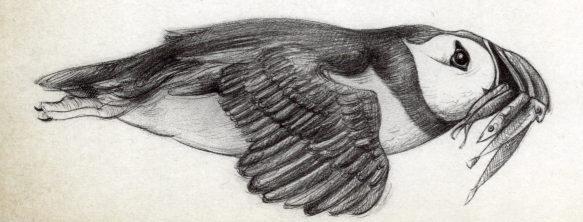

a young puffin chick

Essential facts

↔ **SIZE:** These cute little creatures are roughly 30cm from top to tail.

🏠 **HOME:** Puffins most commonly make their nests in places where predators can't find them. To avoid mammals like rats and foxes, the puffin will set up home on offshore islands – building their nests in the steep, grassy banks of cliffs or among rocks. They spend the winter out at sea, away from land predators.

🍴 **DIET:** Considering where they like to nest, it's no surprise that a puffin's diet consists mostly of fish taken from the sea.

🎂 **LIFE:** A puffin's lifespan is typically about twenty years.

Puffins' feet are webbed to help them swim

Short-Eared Owl

(Asio flammeus)

IRISH NAME: Ulchabhán réisc
CLASS: Aves

With the ability to turn its head 270 degrees around, the short-eared owl has what's almost a superpower. Of course, the owl doesn't use this power for eavesdropping or cheating at cards. Instead it comes in very handy for tracking its prey, since it's much harder to lose sight of your dinner when you can turn your head in every direction.

This bird is one of nature's finest actors. Not that it's fond of movies, but the adult owl will use a touch of drama to protect its young. If a potential predator gets close to the owl's nest, our quick-thinking actor will fake an injury such as a broken wing. Posing as a temptingly easy lunch, the owl will then lead the predator as far away from the nest as possible, before dropping the act and making a quick escape.

The short-eared is the type of owl you're most likely to find in this country. Unlike other owls, this one likes to get out and about during the day, and is also rather quiet. So you won't hear any hooting or whoo-whooing. Instead, the short-eared owl spends the majority of its time looking silently around, taking in the sights and sounds.

Most of the short-eared owls you see in Ireland are tourists. They travel tremendous distances each year to get here from places like Russia and Scandinavia, to where they will return in the spring, when the breeding season comes around again.

Essential facts

SIZE: The short-eared owl is usually between 35 and 45cm long, and has a wingspan of up to 110cm. As is the case with most birds of prey, the female is usually slightly bigger than the male.

HOME: The short-eared owl nests on the ground, scraping a hole from the earth and lining it with comfortable feathers.

DIET: Using fence-posts and trees for surveillance, the short-eared owl keeps its eyes peeled for prey to feed on – mostly rodents, but also insects and even smaller birds.

LIFE: Short-eared owls can live for up to ten years.

European Herring Gull

(Larus argentatus)

IRISH NAME: Faoileán scadán
CLASS: Aves

Look here – I'm not going to beat around the bush. I don't much like herring gulls. They're awfully bossy things. They act like they own the place, as if they're entitled to everything they set their eyes on. Like school bullies, if they spy you eating something they fancy, they're quite likely to make a lunge for it. This is why I'm so protective of my ice-cream on visits to the seaside.

Herring gulls can frequently be spotted tapping their feet menacingly on the ground, as if they're part of some sort of street gang, looking for trouble. Of course, they're just looking for worms. The tapping brings the worms to the surface of the soil, where the gulls happily snack on them. However, I can't help suspecting the gulls aren't quite happy with worms, and would still prefer to be eating my ice-cream.

Since they spend a lot of time at sea, it's no surprise that herring gulls find themselves drinking a good bit of seawater. They have a special gland above their eyes which allows them to filter the salt out from the seawater they drink. You can often see the unwanted salty residue hanging from the end of a gull's beak, as if it's suffering from a runny nose.

Essential facts

 SIZE: The herring gull can grow to 60cm long with a wingspan of 144cm.

 HOME: From cliffs to islands to seaside towns, gulls are commonly found nesting together in large colonies near the sea.

 DIET: Herring gulls are happy to scavenge whatever they can find to eat – rooting through bins and dumps and busy streets, searching for something tasty. Don't think that they're too lazy to catch their dinner, though – the gull is also a predator, mostly of fish.

LIFE: The sturdy gull is quite resourceful, and can last for up to twelve years.

Ask any Dubliner where most of Ireland's seagulls live, and they'd probably say 'this city'. Well, they're not too far wrong – the biggest herring-gull colony in the country is on Lambay island, just off the north Dublin coast.

Eurasian Pygmy Shrew

(Sorex minutus)

IRISH NAME: Dallóg fhraoigh
CLASS: Mammalia

It is polite, when discussing the pygmy shrew, to speak very quietly, in soft tones, little more than a whisper. The pygmy shrew, you see, is very frightened. Of what? Of everything. Tiny, practically blind, and with a list of predators as long as a gibbon's arm, it never ceases to amaze me that the pygmy shrew has survived well enough to become so common in Ireland.

Perhaps due to their poor eyesight or perhaps their general scaredy-cat attitude, young pygmy shrews sometimes form a 'caravan' when moving around. I do not mean the kind of motor-home you see near the beach. This kind of 'caravan' means the way pygmy shrews move together in a line. With the mother shrew taking the lead, each baby shrew holds onto the tail of the one in front to ensure that no one gets lost. It's quite a sight, like a small furry train shuffling along through the grass, or a nervous group of humans dancing the conga at a wedding.

Being awfully tiny and therefore not very good in a fight, the pygmy shrew has developed a different kind of defence mechanism. If it's challenged by a predator, the pygmy shrew will release an unpleasant smell, making the predator stop to reconsider whether it really wants to make this stinky little creature its lunch.

> The primary habitat of the fearful pygmy shrew is 'in hiding'. Hiding in a hedge, hiding in a bush, hiding in dense vegetation in the woods ...

> Some pygmy shrews have bright red teeth. This bright red colouring comes about because the pygmy shrew's teeth are rich in iron – which gives them protection from wear and tear.

Essential facts

↔ **SIZE:** Measuring between 4.5 and 6cm in length, with a tail that can be as long as 5cm, the pygmy shrew is Ireland's tiniest mammal.

🏠 **HOME:** These small, mouse-like creatures are found in many different locations across the countryside, always on the lookout for somewhere they can make a nest of dry grass and hide away to protect themselves.

🍴 **DIET:** The pygmy shrew is a hungry little creature, eating one and a quarter times its body-weight in food a day. A big fan of bugs like spiders, wood-lice and beetles, the pygmy shrew needs so much food that even two hours without a meal and it can starve!

This means that the pygmy shrew must stay awake all day and all night on a constant search for snacks, taking just short naps between meals.

🎂 **LIFE:** Life can be difficult for this poor little thing, and the average lifespan of a pygmy shrew in Ireland is only around a year. A lot can happen in a year, though – pygmy shrews breed terribly fast, so can end up having twenty or more babies.

These little animals are rather a common sight in Ireland, but while you might see a pygmy shrew they're unlikely to see you – they have terrible eyesight.

This is the actual size of a pygmy shrew.

Viviparous Lizard

(*Zootoca vivipara*)

IRISH NAME: Laghairt choiteann
CLASS: Reptilia

I know what you're thinking: *Oh no, has the viviparous lizard got lost on its way somewhere else? Surely a lizard shouldn't be in Ireland!*

Well, yes, this *is* the one and only lizard that calls this island home. And true enough, the viviparous lizard seems not quite to know what it's doing here. It darts around quickly from rock to rock, never appearing to stay in the one place, always looking like it has somewhere else it needs to be.

Lizards need sun, and Ireland, for all its many plusses, is not a great place for getting a tan. So the lizard spends most of autumn and winter in hibernation, only appearing when the weather begins to get warmer.

There are plenty of predators who see the viviparous lizard as a rather exotic meal. Birds in particular are quite fond of the idea of this scaly creature as a lunch item. However, the viviparous lizard is often two steps ahead. It has mastered the amazing ability of leaving part of its body behind as it scuttles away. Any bird impolite enough to try to eat the lizard is often left with nothing more than a beakful of tail – and the lizard can immediately start getting down to the business of growing a brand-new tail as a replacement.

'Viviparous' means that this lizard gives birth to live young, rather than laying eggs like other reptiles. The mother lizard keeps the eggs inside her body for safekeeping, and baby lizards hatch while they're still inside their mother. When they're ready to be born, the little lizards come out – without any shell!

Essential facts

↔ **SIZE:** Ireland's only reptile, the viviparous lizard (or common lizard) is usually between 10 and 16cm long.

🏠 **HOME:** The viviparous lizard can be found in a range of habitats, including woods, bogs and sand dunes. It can mostly be spotted in places where it can bask in the sun, such as the surface of a rock or log. They like to have a place to scurry away into when there is danger, and at night-time they will have a favourite spot where they can take shelter.

🍴 **DIET:** A keen hunter of slugs, earthworms, spiders, and other insects, the viviparous lizard will stun its prey by pouncing on it, then swallow it up in one bite.

🎂 **LIFE:** The viviparous lizard usually lives to around five years of age.

Western European Hedgehog

(Erinaceus europaeus)

IRISH NAME: Gráinneog
CLASS: Mammalia

Hedgehogs are prickly little creatures. They start off with baby spikes or spines, but eventually these will fall out and be replaced by grown-up spines. This process, called 'quilling', is rather similar to what happens when we humans shed our baby teeth in order to grow adult teeth.

Back in the old days the world wasn't so scary for hedgehogs. They pottered merrily around at a slow pace, safe in the knowledge that they had a good form of protection against predators. If a fox (for example) were to come upon a hedgehog and fancy having it for dinner, the hedgehog would simply curl up in a ball, and its spikes would stand a decent chance of putting the fox off.

Unfortunately, the world has changed an awful lot since the hedgehog got its spikes. If it finds itself in danger when crossing the road, the rolling-into-a-ball trick – though still impressive – is not very effective.

The hedgehog's spikes may not stand much of a chance against cars or trucks, but luckily the hedgehog has another thing going for it: it's a nocturnal animal, which is to say that it mostly comes out at night. This is quite fortunate, because it means that the hedgehog is less likely to encounter the kind of heavy traffic that humans face on the way to school or work.

> I have been unable to establish, however, whether hedgehogs have a prickly version of the Tooth Fairy.

Essential facts

↔ **SIZE:** This prickly little creature is about 25cm in length.

🏠 **HOME:** The Western European hedgehog doesn't build a permanent home, but instead sleeps in 'day nests', which are usually piles of leaves, in hedges, woods, or the occasional garden.

🍴 **DIET:** Spiders, caterpillars, beetles, and other insects make up most of the hedgehog's menu.

🎂 **LIFE:** A Western European hedgehog can live for up to ten years. Unfortunately, many hedgehogs have their lives cut off rather younger than that, because of us human beings and our cars.

A hedgehog that has curled into a ball to protect itself

You wouldn't think that the slow and sleepy hedgehog would have much in common with the fast and fickle bat, but these two creatures are the only Irish mammals that truly hibernate for the winter.

26

Red Squirrel

(Sciurus vulgaris)

IRISH NAME: Iora rua
CLASS: Mammalia

Everybody loves an underdog. The kind of character who really shouldn't stand a chance when coming up against someone bigger, louder, and more aggressive. The red squirrel is most definitely an underdog, as it finds itself being overwhelmed by its brute of a cousin, the grey squirrel.

This grey bully of a squirrel arrived in Ireland in 1911 and immediately started to take over. The red squirrel was smaller and quieter as well as redder – and it quickly found itself in competition for food and territory. What's more, the grey squirrel brought with it a disease that killed off a lot of red squirrels.

While the red squirrel lives in relative harmony with the woodland it calls home, the grey squirrel tends to leave the place in an awful state, brazenly stomping around, tearing bark off trees, and generally being a bit of a nuisance.

Despite its problems with bullies, the red squirrel population in Ireland is still rather healthy. So there's hope for the underdog (or the undersquirrel) yet.

By comparison with tails in other parts of the animal kingdom, squirrel tails might strike you as rather over the top. However, I assure you that squirrels are not simply trying to show off. As well as making the squirrel look fabulous, its bushy tail is very important for balance, particularly when jumping from tree to tree.

Their tails also play a part in how squirrels communicate with one another. When there is danger nearby, for example, a squirrel can let other squirrels know by flicking its tail. And when the weather is cold the squirrel's tail can work very well as a makeshift blanket.

> The red squirrel is not a fan of the winter, but it doesn't quite hibernate. Instead it spends as much time as it possibly can at home, wandering out occasionally to stock up from the three-month supply of food that it's hidden away somewhere nearby.

Essential facts

SIZE: A red squirrel can grow as tall as 25cm, with its tail being just about that length again.

HOME: A squirrel's nest is called a drey, and is usually made of sticks and leaves which are placed high up in a tree, leaning against the trunk – or in a hollow of the tree itself.

DIET: The most popular category of food on a squirrel's menu is nuts and seeds. Squirrels are very good at long-term planning, and they hide supplies of food throughout the year so they'll have plenty to keep themselves full during the winter. This is where the phrase 'to squirrel something away' comes from.

LIFE: Red squirrels can live for up to six years.

As the seasons change, a red squirrel's fur may lose its reddishness, but you can still tell them from grey squirrels by the tufts of fur that red squirrels have on the tops of their ears.

Irish Hare

(Lepus timidus hibernicus)

IRISH NAME: Giorria
CLASS: Mammalia

The Irish hare is only found in Ireland, and is not to be confused with Irish hair, which is only found on Irish people.

A close relative of the European mountain hare, it's no surprise that Irish hares can be found quite commonly near mountain peaks. However, unlike other mountain hares, some of our Irish hares have moved down from the mountains, all the way to sea level. So you can also find them on lowland pastures.

This marvellous creature is one of the oldest inhabitants of this island, having been here since before the last ice age.

Though they look quite similar, a hare and a rabbit are very different animals. They are indeed related, but hares are far bigger, have longer ears, and prefer a solitary life. Put it this way: you can make a pet of a rabbit, but a hare would be a very different matter.

In snowier climates, hares often go white in winter, for camouflage. The Irish hare, however, usually stays brown all year round, because our snowy days are few and far between.

In the springtime, the hare world goes a little crazy. This is the breeding season, and hares get up to all sorts of antics in the name of mating. They run around even more than usual, with females leading males on a chase to see which one is the fastest, and even like to box. No wonder we use the phrase 'mad as a March hare'.

Male and female hares boxing

A baby hare or 'leveret'

Essential facts

↔ **SIZE:** The Irish hare grows to a length of roughly 45 to 65cm, and when fully grown can weigh anything from 3 to 6kg. Female Irish hares are slightly larger than males.

HOME: Unlike rabbits, the hare does not live in a warren but in a 'form', which is a little patch of flattened vegetation hidden under heather and long grass.

DIET: Hares mostly eat heather, grasses, and herbs (wild, grassy herbs – not the kind that humans use for cooking dinner), and are known to eat their own droppings to get as much nutrition as possible from every meal.

LIFE: The Irish hare can live for up to nine years.

Because hares have an eye on each side of their head, they have a field of vision close to 360 degrees. That means they can see almost everything around them, so there's no point trying to sneak up on one.

Eurasian Otter

(Lutra lutra)

IRISH NAME: Dobharchú
CLASS: Mammalia

As a mammal that spends quite a lot of time in the water, the otter has a list of swimming advantages that a human Olympic swimmer might be very jealous of. Not only do otters have webbed feet and claws to help them move quickly through the water, but they can also close their ears and nose to stop water from getting in when they're diving. They also have a dense layer of fur under their water-resistant hair which keeps them nice and cosy while swimming.

You don't usually see otters out in the open. They spend their day hidden away in their homes (called holts), waiting for night to fall. That's when they venture out to patrol their territory, which could be as large as several square kilometres and contain a number of holts belonging to the same otter. The otter moves from holt to holt, checking in, hiding out, making sure everything is safe and its territory is secure.

Otters scurry around through tunnels and other types of cover, which is another reason they are not very visible. Even when they are out in the open, they are mostly camouflaged with thick brown hair!

From what we have seen of otters, we know that they love to play. From sliding down muddy banks into the water, to fiddling with pebbles, to chasing one another around, this creature knows how to unwind. Of course, the best games are the ones where you learn something useful in the process, and many of the skills that otters use when playing come in rather handy when they're out hunting for food.

There are many different types of otter around the world that are considered endangered species, but luckily our Eurasian otter (also known as the 'common otter') has a healthy population here in Ireland.

There are estimated to be around ten thousand otters in Ireland, which is quite a lot. Nevertheless, they're rather private animals, so if you spot one, consider yourself lucky.

Essential facts

↔ **SIZE:** The Eurasian otter can grow to be up to 96cm. Add a handsome tail of 35 to 45cm to that and a lot of otters can be well over a metre long.

🏠 **HOME:** These furry mammals are semi-aquatic, which means they like the water. They're found in rivers, streams, lakes, and sometimes even on the beach, always living in homes they've built themselves, called holts.

🍴 **DIET:** Eurasian otters are big fans of fish, particularly salmon, trout, and smaller fish like sticklebacks.

🎂 **LIFE:** Most Eurasian otters live for around five years, but some have been known to live for twice that long.

Mother otters lie on their backs in the water and hold their pups on their front.

Baby otter, called a pup

32

European Badger
(Meles meles)

IRISH NAME: Broc
CLASS: Mammalia

> Ireland has one of the world's healthiest populations of badgers – even though the poor things have an awfully hard time dealing with angry farmers and our love of cars.

Badgers have a reputation for being particularly fierce and dangerous. It's true that they're bulky and strong and have scary teeth, but actually they are rather shy and usually quite placid beasts. They like to keep out of sight, ambling about at night looking for food or busying away below the ground.

A sett, which is what we call a badger's home, is far more than just a comfy hole in the ground. In fact, if you were to pick one animal to build you a house, you could do a lot worse than ask a badger. The level of construction on setts can be really quite breathtaking, with different rooms for different badgers to sleep in. They have more than one way in or out, which helps to avoid traffic jams and provides quick escape routes in case of emergency.

With homes that are the animal equivalent of a palace or a mansion, it's no surprise that badgers are very house-proud. Perhaps you've been told at some point that you shouldn't eat in bed because you'll get crumbs everywhere? Well, badgers agree: even though they regularly change their bedding (dragging in fresh straw and dry grass by pulling it along with their chin) badgers still won't bring food back to eat in the sett. How very sensible!

When they need to go to the toilet, they most certainly won't be doing that indoors either. Instead, they make their way out to specially built shallow pits that are placed at the edge of their territory, far enough from the sett that they won't have to put up with any bad smells when they are at home.

Essential facts

 SIZE: The European badger is usually around a metre in length, and ranges in weight from about 7 to 13kg, though it tends to get a bit heavier – up to around 17kg – when cold weather is on the way.

 HOME: Badgers are excellent diggers and live in large networks of underground tunnels called 'setts'.

DIET: A European badger's menu can feature a wide selection of treats, from worms to bumblebees to frogs, and from bugs to nuts to fruit and veg. Even sometimes a small mammal like a mouse or rabbit.

 LIFE: Sadly, many badger cubs don't make it through their first year – but if they do they'll often live up to the age of six. However, it's not unheard of for badgers to live as much as ten years longer than that.

Even though the badgers we have in Ireland belong to the same species as those across the Irish Sea in Britain, British badgers are fussier than Irish ones. In Britain, badgers are quite protective of their homes, and aren't very happy when neighbouring badgers arrive by on a visit. Irish badgers, on the other hand, are very sociable, and pop in and out of each other's homes all the time.

34

Red Fox
(Vulpes vulpes)

IRISH NAME: Madra rua
CLASS: Mammalia

Country life is often slower and more relaxed than city life, and this seems to suit most animals. But the red fox feels just as much at home in the hustle and bustle of the city as in a sleepy part of the countryside.

The urban fox always seems to be in the know. It can seek out the most obscure and desirable locations for setting up a home (or a den, as it's called). From a garden shed to a compost heap, the red fox finds all the best places to be. Even a hard-to-reach garage roof could provide a home for the wandering fox, since it's a pretty good climber, too.

By far their favourite places are the ones where they can find a good supply of food – from bins, or generous humans who leave out scraps in the hope of making a new friend. Foxes do appreciate a free meal, but I wouldn't get your hopes up for a life of fun and games with your new pet fox – a fox may look like a particularly dapper dog but they are far shyer and much more independent than dogs.

Foxes tend to avoid large open spaces, since they always like to keep a hiding place, some cover, or a quick escape route close at hand. This is why foxes in rural areas will often be found near farmlands or woods. Unlike some of their relatives, foxes don't like to go around in packs, and instead are happier when going off on their own. The happy exception to this is when baby foxes (called 'kits') arrive. A fox family is a very tightly knit unit, and both parents will stick together with the kits for months, until the kits are ready to start going on adventures by themselves.

Ireland has no shortage of red foxes, and they can be found in every county in the country.

a young fox kit

Essential facts

 SIZE: Red foxes can grow to 1.5m in length, with half of that being made up of an elegant tail. Male foxes, (called dogs) are larger than the female foxes.

 HOME: The red fox isn't terribly fussy about where it lives. It's happy setting up a den in the woods, in the open countryside, or in suburban areas of towns or cities.

DIET: Another thing the fox isn't fussy about is its diet. They eat meat, hunting chickens, mice and rats, rabbits, or small hares, amongst other creatures. When the hunting isn't going too well they're happy to scavenge for whatever they can find, eating fruit, insects, or leftovers that they can find in your bins.

 LIFE: An Irish red fox will usually live for four to six years.

Red Deer

(Cervus elaphus)

IRISH NAME: Fia rua
CLASS: Mammalia

The red deer is a noble creature. It seems like an animal that would be well suited to being a lord or a lady, if such things existed in the animal world. With a fine, reddish-brown coat and a streak of white down its chest, it's the kind of animal that makes you feel like you should immediately drop everything and paint its portrait.

The most majestic of all is the male red deer, or stag, who grows from his forehead a tremendous crown of antlers that seems to stretch up to the sky. Oh, how dignified! How glorious! Well, no, not really. Because what do these stags do with their antlers? They fight with them.

You see, stags are always trying to impress the hinds, or female red deer, and one guaranteed way of impressing them is to be the biggest stag. When two stags find themselves competing for the affection of a hind, they first have a roaring contest to see who has the biggest roar. This is usually followed by a 'parallel walk' where they size each other up. If after that they still can't tell who's bigger, they resort to a fight. The stags duck their heads so that their antlers are pointing out, then run straight at one another. With their antlers locked together, the two males huff and puff, heaving forward like in a rugby scrum, trying to prove that they are the biggest and the strongest. When one stag eventually wins out, he may chase his defeated opponent away.

One of Ireland's oldest residents, the red deer is believed to have been roaming this island since 10,000 BCE.

Essential facts

 SIZE: As Ireland's largest land mammal, a male red deer (or stag) can stand an impressive 1.2m tall – and that's not counting his antlers. Female red deer stand a little shorter, averaging about 1m to the shoulder.

HOME: Red deer love the forest, but will often move between the woods and more open grassland. As wooded areas have become scarcer, deer have found themselves living in places they wouldn't otherwise have chosen, such as wetlands and moors.

 DIET: Like cows and sheep, red deer mainly graze on grass, but when the cold weather rolls in they'll fill up on moss, heather shoots, and the thick, chewy mat-grass that can be found on moors and mountaintops.

 LIFE: A red deer in Ireland will live on average for thirteen to sixteen years.

Natterjack Toad

(Epidalea calamita)

IRISH NAME: Buaf natterjack
CLASS: Amphibia

The natterjack toad is the rarest of Ireland's three amphibian species – 'amphibian' meaning that it can live and breathe both on land and in water. Our other two amphibian species are the smooth newt and the common frog.

Natterjacks love to live near the sea. Global warming has led to rising sea-levels, which is bad news for the natterjack toad. Its favourite places to live are being flooded with seawater. With fewer and fewer places to call home, the natterjack was in real danger of becoming extinct in Ireland, and at one point became a very rare sight indeed.

Things have improved for the natterjack, however! Garden ponds have become quite fashionable – a trend that's proved convenient for natterjack toads, since these ponds have created ideal habitats for them. As a result, the natterjack population has bounced back, and we're now seeing far more of them than we have for years.

The toad is a close relative of the frog, an amphibian well known for hopping around. However, the only way you could make a natterjack toad hop is if you accidentally dropped one on a trampoline. This is because the natterjack has much shorter legs than a frog, so it sticks to crawling from place to place instead.

You can spot natterjack eggs in the springtime, in streams and woodland pools. They are a bit like frogspawn, but strung together like a string made of jelly, woven throughout vegetation. Once hatched, the baby toads, or tadpoles, start to grow arms and legs. Within about twelve weeks they transform into fully grown toads.

Tadpoles

Essential facts

↔ **SIZE:** The natterjack toad is usually around 6 to 7cm in length.

HOME: This toad is found in sandy or marshy areas near the sea.

DIET: When fully grown, natterjack toads love eating insects, and since they have a very long tongue, they're pretty nifty at catching them.

LIFE: Including all stages of their lives, natterjack toads can live for up to fifteen years.

A natterjack using its long tongue to catch its dinner

The name 'natterjack' means chattering toad – the jack (or toad) that natters – because their call is not only particularly loud, but also goes on all summer.

Purple Sea Urchin

(Strongylocentrotus purpuratus)

IRISH NAME: Cuán mara corcra
CLASS: Echinoidea

Like a prickly purple furball with a mind of its own, the purple sea urchin is as close to an alien as I've ever seen.

It looks a bit like a Christmas-tree decoration, or one of those things you find in your grandmother's living room that releases a nice smell every hour or so.

This is no decoration, however – and it definitely doesn't release pleasant perfumes. And (thankfully) you don't have to go to the moon to meet one – you just have to have a root around in a rock pool by the sea.

Inside this delightfully flamboyant shell lives a delicate invertebrate that's an established local resident on the west coast of Ireland. The purple sea urchin can move about, using its spines (which is what scientists call their prickly spikes) and its long tube-legs, which are hidden in amongst the spines.

With its shell covered in spines, you might think that the purple sea urchin looks like a hedgehog that's coloured its hair and moved under the sea. Of course, a hedgehog would never do that, but someone else might have had that same thought in the past, since the word 'urchin' is actually an old-fashioned way of saying 'hedgehog'.

A sea urchin's spines seen close-up

An invertebrate is a small creature without a backbone (or indeed any bones at all), such as a snail or an octopus.

Even if you don't manage to find a living purple sea urchin, their shells quite regularly wash up on the shore (thankfully without the sharp spines).

a sea urchin's shell

Essential facts

SIZE: The shell (known as the 'test') of the purple sea urchin can be up to 7cm wide, and is covered in prickly spines and long 'tube legs' which work to pull it along.

HOME: The purple sea urchin is quite at home on the ocean floor, but it is usually found in shallow waters near the coast. Keep your eyes peeled the next time you're exploring tide pools near the sea shore – you may well spy a purple sea urchin clinging to the rocks.

DIET: At the base of the test you'll find the purple sea urchin's mouth – usually surrounded by five sharp and strong teeth which they use to eat algae, kelp (a type of seaweed), and even small crustaceans.

LIFE: The purple sea urchin has been known to live for up to fifty years.

Three-Spined Stickleback

(Gasterosteus aculeatus)

IRISH NAME: Garmachán
CLASS: Actinopterygii

You have to admire the stickleback for trying. This tiny little fish found itself way down near the bottom of the food chain, perfectly suited to becoming a tasty meal for all sorts of animals – but the plucky stickleback has developed several ways of putting up a good fight.

Unlike most fish, the stickleback does not have scales, but several plates of armour instead, like a medieval knight or a modern tank. For the armoured stickleback, the best form of defence is attack. At the first sign of a predator, such as a larger fish, two or more sticklebacks will approach their challenger as a team and goad the larger fish.

This tactic is sometimes successful, but even when it's not and the courageous little fish ends up in the mouth of its attacker, the stickleback still has one trick left up its fishy sleeve. It's equipped with three spikes along its back for just this sort of occasion. Ouch!

If every year all the fish in the ocean gathered together to hold an award ceremony for 'Father of the Year', the male stickleback would certainly win. Before a single egg has even arrived, the male stickleback busies himself making a roofed nest from bits of seaweed and other plants. Then once the nest is filled with eggs, the father will guard the eggs fiercely until they've hatched, allowing Mum to head off, presumably for a well-earned break.

In Ireland we have two distinct species of stickleback. The most common is the three-spined stickleback – which, contrary to its name, often has four spines. The other is the nine-spined stickleback, which can have between eight and ten spines. How confusing!

Essential facts

 SIZE: These are very small fish, with not many of them growing bigger than 7cm in length.

HOME: From lakes to ponds, rivers to streams, and even in the sea near the shore, three-spined sticklebacks can be found in most bodies of water in Ireland. Your best bet for seeing one up close is to take a nose around rock pools on the sea shore.

 DIET: Even though the stickleback is a small fish, it has no problem being a carnivore, and it feasts on even smaller creatures like insects and fish larvae (very young fish).

 LIFE: The lifespan of a three-spined stickleback can vary widely, from one to four years.

A stickleback protecting his nest

44

Common Hermit Crab

(Pagurus bernhardus)

IRISH NAME: Faocha ghliomaigh
CLASS: Malacostraca

Crabs and shells, you might think, go together like books and pages, trees and leaves, ice-cream and cones – the very thought of one without the other seems positively silly. Yet the hermit crab has the misfortune to be exactly that very odd thing: a crab without a shell.

This means that the poor old hermit crab is terribly vulnerable to the outside world, so it has had to come up with its own solution. As soon as it possibly can, it nabs the nearest empty seashell and sets up home inside.

If there isn't a suitable seashell handy, a hermit crab can make do with any old thing it finds, such as a tin can or a plastic cup.

Snug as it may be in its stolen home, the hermit crab does from time to time feel the need for a change, especially if it has grown too big for its old shell. Sometimes one crab can take a liking to another crab's shell – in which case it may start a fight in the hope of getting an upgrade. The fighting crab has a particular trick it can use in a sticky situation. If a hermit crab finds itself being pulled out of its shell by an attacker, it can 'throw a leg', meaning it simply abandons the leg that the other crab is pulling on and makes a quick getaway!

I'm pleased to report, though, that hermit crabs don't always resort to fighting about shells. They can also find a new home through cooperation. If one crab stumbles across a nice new shell that isn't quite right for them, it will often wait around for another crab to come along. It knows that if this new arrival takes a fancy to the vacant shell, they'll leave behind their old home for the first crab to move into. Up to twenty crabs have been known to form an orderly queue, all waiting for the chance to trade up to the shell left behind by the crab in front of them.

> The common hermit crab has a rather large set of front claws, but both claws are not the same size – one is much bigger than the other. The bigger claw is used for hunting, fighting, and even as a front door for its shell. The smaller one is mostly used for scooping up food.

A hermit crab without a shell, in the process of moving house

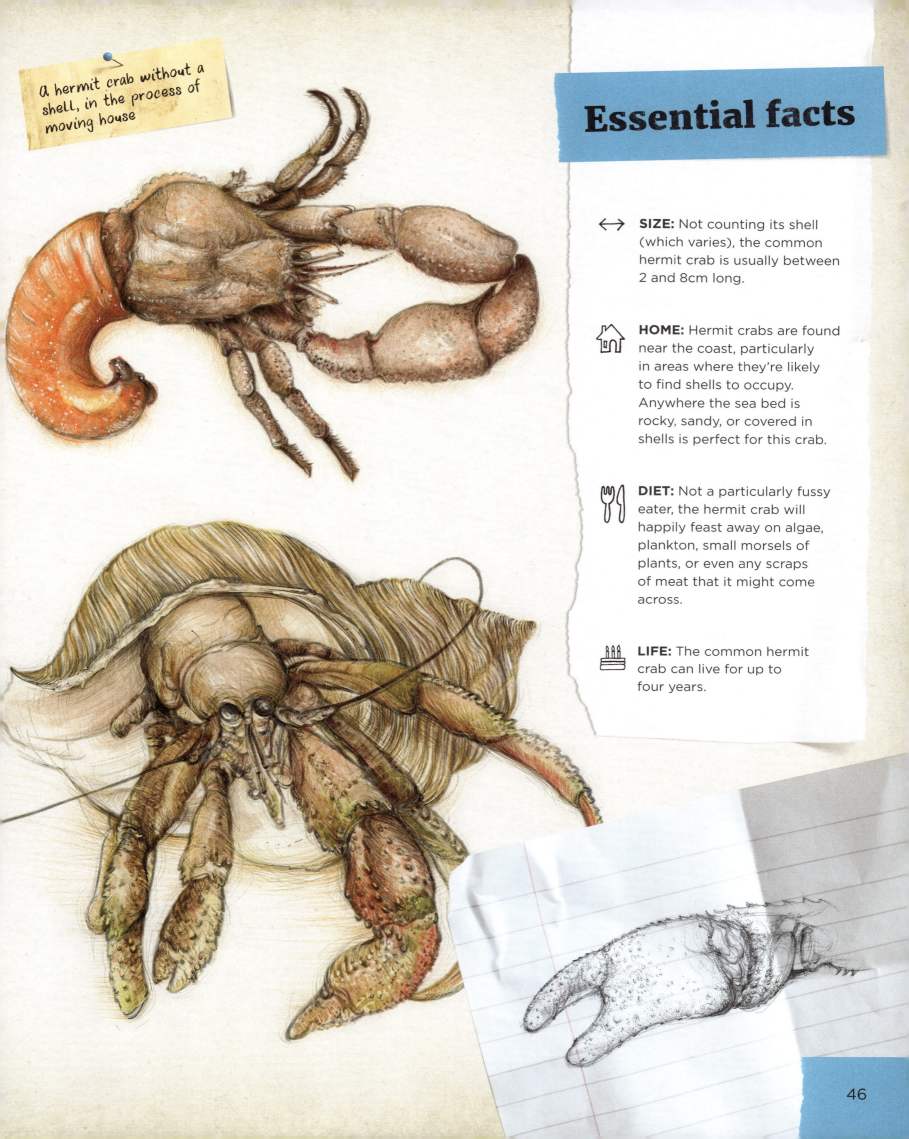

Essential facts

↔ **SIZE:** Not counting its shell (which varies), the common hermit crab is usually between 2 and 8cm long.

🏠 **HOME:** Hermit crabs are found near the coast, particularly in areas where they're likely to find shells to occupy. Anywhere the sea bed is rocky, sandy, or covered in shells is perfect for this crab.

🍴 **DIET:** Not a particularly fussy eater, the hermit crab will happily feast away on algae, plankton, small morsels of plants, or even any scraps of meat that it might come across.

🎂 **LIFE:** The common hermit crab can live for up to four years.

Atlantic Salmon
(Salmo salar)

IRISH NAME: Bradán Atlantach
CLASS: Actinopterygii

There are many things about the Atlantic salmon that are rather incredible. For one thing: most fish are either sea fish or freshwater fish, but the salmon manages to be both, spending some time in lakes and rivers and some time at sea.

From its home in the rivers and lakes of Ireland, the salmon swims all the way out to the depths of the Atlantic Ocean, where it will hang around for a few years before turning around and swimming all the way back again to the very river it was born in.

The salmon is not going on a strange sort of holiday, though. It makes its way to the ocean to grow. The open ocean is the best place for the salmon to feed to its heart's content, getting as big as it possibly can before returning home to spawn (lay eggs) and start the process all over again.

Salmon do not carry maps or phones, and they are not particularly good at asking for directions. So how do they manage to travel thousands of kilometres back to the exact same river they were born in?

The answer is at least partly due to something called 'olfactory memory', which means memory of smells. So no matter how far these intrepid travellers go, no matter how big their adventure becomes, they still remember the smell of home.

Sometimes the returning salmon can find the way home blocked by obstacles on the river, such as dams or generators or waterfalls. Humans are often the ones responsible for putting these obstacles there in the first place, so to make up for the inconvenience (and help the returning fish make their way back upriver) fish ladders are put in place. These water-covered stairways allow salmon and other fish to leap upwards, one step at a time, and bypass obstacles that would otherwise have cut their amazing journey short.

> Another fish with the rare ability to live in either fresh or salt water is the stickleback.

Salmon travelling upstream

Essential facts

↔ **SIZE:** When fully grown, the Atlantic salmon's average length is around 70cm, and it can weigh anything from 3 to 5kg.

🏠 **HOME:** When Atlantic salmon come home from their years at sea, they make shallow nests in the gravel beds of their home rivers. Here the eggs are laid and the baby salmon hatch and spend their early lives.

🍴 **DIET:** Young Atlantic salmon eat mostly plankton, but when they venture out to sea the salmon bulk up with shrimp, squid, and smaller fish like herring.

🎂 **LIFE:** Over the course of three to eight years the Atlantic salmon goes by many different names. Once hatched from the egg, a salmon will grow into a fry (a very small fish), then a parr, which is well suited to freshwater. Before visiting the sea, they will change into a smolt, and once they've returned from their adventure and spawned they are called kelts.

The salmon plays a major role in Irish mythology. The Salmon of Knowledge was a magical salmon which gave great powers of wisdom to the Irish hero Fionn mac Cumhaill when he (accidentally) tasted the fish while cooking it.

Common Seal

(Phoca vitulina)

IRISH NAME: Rón beag
CLASS: Mammalia

Ireland is lucky enough to have two kinds of seal – the grey seal and the common seal. They are very similar in appearance, but if you want to tell them apart, it's good to remember that the common seal is usually the smaller of the two species.

Grey seals are of course grey, but common seals are also usually (and unhelpfully) greyish. Both kinds of seal have a fetching pattern of spots on their backs. They also have webbed 'fingers' on their fore-flippers and rather nasty little claws, which they sometimes use for fighting, but mostly for scratching themselves.

With sleek bodies like torpedoes or submarines, it's no surprise that seals are magnificent swimmers. Not only are they incredibly fast when moving through the water, but they can swim at great speed over very long distances. Seals could live on land if they really wanted to (and in fact they do tend to come ashore when they are ready to mate and have babies) but they spend most of their lives at sea.

Since they spend so much time in the water, seals need a clever way of keeping warm. They fight off the cold with a special double layer of warmth: an incredibly toasty layer of protective fat, called blubber, which they hide underneath their furry skin.

The seal's massive whiskers are much more than a fashion statement. Since it's not terribly easy to see or hear underwater, seals use their whiskers to detect movements like the flow of fish passing through the water nearby.

This skill can be very convenient, not just at mealtimes, but also when swimming in the dark. Scientists have even found that due to these incredible whiskers, seals are able to find their way around the place while wearing a blindfold!

> In human terms, this is a bit like wearing pyjamas under your school uniform, and not too far away from what my mother used to call her 'favourite winter coat', which was really just two coats.

Essential facts

 SIZE: The common seal averages a little under 2m in length, with the males being slightly larger than the females. Their bodies are very bulky, because of all the blubber under their fur.

 HOME: Common seals can be found all along the coastline of Ireland. They're happier closer to shore, near beaches or inlets, relaxing on islands or rocky outcrops.

 DIET: There are plenty of things in the sea that seals consider delicious, from shoals of fish like mackerel, to squid, octopus, and shellfish.

LIFE: Female seals have a longer life expectancy than males, usually living to the age of around thirty-two – which is a good six years older than the males.

With sleek and powerful bodies, seals can work up quite some speed when they get going – hitting speeds of up to twenty-five knots which, on land, is around forty-six kilometres per hour.

A baby seal

50

Bottlenose Dolphin

(*Tursiops truncatus*)

IRISH NAME: Deilf bholgshrónach
CLASS: Mammalia

If the animal kingdom held exams like the ones we have in schools, I suspect that everyone would be queueing up to copy the answers from the dolphins. These fascinating and friendly creatures are *incredibly* intelligent. They even have their own form of language, communicating with one another through a series of clicks, whistles, and chirps.

Dolphins travel around together in groups called 'pods', which are sometimes sort of like a family, and sometimes sort of like a gang. Like any gang of friends, dolphin pods spend a lot of time playing – and are even known to play with humans when it takes their fancy.

Having a group of friends about also comes in handy for catching fish. Dolphin pods have been known to click and whistle a plan together like a sports team before a match, then set an elaborate trap to catch enough food for everyone.

If you went to sea without your glasses, and spotted a dolphin in the distance, you'd be forgiven if you exclaimed, 'Oh, look, a really big fish!' Dolphins do look a bit like fish, but they are in fact mammals – which means (amongst other things) that they breathe air. The bottlenose dolphin can spend up to seven minutes holding its breath underwater, but then it has to return to the surface to breathe, not through its mouth, but through a blow-hole at the top of its head.

Dolphins rely a great deal on sound. They can learn a lot about their surroundings by making noises. The sound waves of their clicks and whistles bounce off things in the dolphins' environment, and then bounce right back to them – letting them know what's there.

Dolphins and whales are aquatic mammals, so unlike fish they give birth to live babies, rather than laying eggs.

Essential facts

↔ **SIZE:** A bottlenose dolphin can be anything from 2m to just over 4m long. Some of the world's biggest bottlenose dolphins are found in the waters around Ireland.

🏠 **HOME:** Dolphins love vast oceans, but bottlenose dolphins are often seen swimming close to the shore.

🍴 **DIET:** The bottlenose dolphin is quite happy munching away on squid, fish, and all manner of shellfish.

🎂 **LIFE:** Male bottlenose dolphins will usually live for around twenty-five to thirty years, but females can live longer, even well into their forties.

Dolphins have a long history of helping out when they spot a human in danger in the water. From fending off angry sharks to leading lost swimmers to safety, there have been many recorded examples of dolphins playing the hero.

Killer Whale
(Orcinus orca)

IRISH NAME: Cráin dhubh
CLASS: Mammalia

When you're as big as a killer whale, the world is a smaller place. Orcas (as they are also called) swim great distances at tremendous depths, no doubt lost in their own thoughts. Like dolphins, these highly intelligent animals travel the oceans with their friends and family in groups called 'pods'. They feast on smaller animals like seals and fish, and never have much problem catching something to eat, because they are excellent hunters.

Killer whales in particular are very fond of a chat. Members of a pod can often be heard calling out to one another, and since these massive animals are capable of making noises as loud as a truck beeping its horn, killer whales can talk to each other even when they're several kilometres apart.

Like dolphins, whales can use echo-location to communicate and to 'see' in murky waters. This means that a killer whale is safe to go exploring and doesn't have to worry too much about getting lost from the rest of the pod.

The name 'killer' is definitely appropriate, but should only strike fear into your heart if you're a seal, a fish, or something else that a killer whale likes to eat for dinner. Humans are, of course, roughly the same size as a seal, but thankfully killer whales have never been known to eat people.

Killer whales are rather nifty dressers. With their sleek black-and-white outfits they look as if they are going out to a formal dinner. But with everyone dressed in the same style, how can you possibly tell one killer whale apart from another? The trick is to look at the subtle differences in their white patches and the shape of their dorsal fins (the fins that stick up from their backs). When it comes to these two parts of the killer-whale uniform, no two orcas are exactly alike.

> You might be surprised to learn that the killer whale is more closely related to dolphins than to other whales!

Essential facts

⟷ **SIZE:** Adult male killer whales can weigh almost 5,500kg, and grow up to 8m long - they're really quite big.

⌂ **HOME:** Though they are happiest in waters that are between about 20 and 60m deep, killer whales will often wander into shallower spots near the coast, usually when they're in search of something to eat.

🍴 **DIET:** As their name implies, killer whales are hunters and eat seals, fish, and dolphins.

🎂 **LIFE:** If they're lucky, killer whales can expect to live to the grand old age of fifty.

Whale's tail

Ireland is known to have at least one pod of killer whales, but they are quite shy, so are not often seen. However, some people have been lucky enough to spot them from whale-watching boats off the south-west coast, and even, on occasion, from the shore.

Basking Shark

(Cetorhinus maximus)

IRISH NAME: Liamhán gréine
CLASS: Chondrichthyes

Basking sharks enjoy cold water. You'll very rarely see them getting anywhere close to the equator, where the water is lovely and warm. Instead they spend most of their time further north and south, and we see quite a lot of them in the waters around Ireland – which are pleasantly cool.

The name 'basking shark' is a bit misleading, because these sharks don't really like to bask in the sun's rays at all. They do spend a lot of time near the surface of the water – which made people think they were basking in the sun. Basking sharks are definitely not up there trying to get a tan, though. In fact, they swim close to the surface because that's the best place for them to feed.

I can assure you that the sharks that we have in Irish waters are nothing like the scary ones you see in films. They do *look* pretty scary though. Basking sharks are huge, and they have extremely large mouths that seem to be open at all times – which, it's fair to say, is an unfortunate look for a friendly shark. The really very innocent reason that the basking shark keeps its mouth open is so that it can constantly filter water for plankton, which is what it likes to eat.

Plankton are tiny sea creatures, about the size of a pinhead. Even at their biggest plankton will only grow up to a centimetre across. So unless you're smaller than a shirt button, you have nothing to be worried about around basking sharks!

The basking shark may be quite large, but the same cannot be said for its brain. In fact, it's got the smallest brain size of any shark, relative to the size of its body. Which means that our friend the basking shark is unusually stupid.

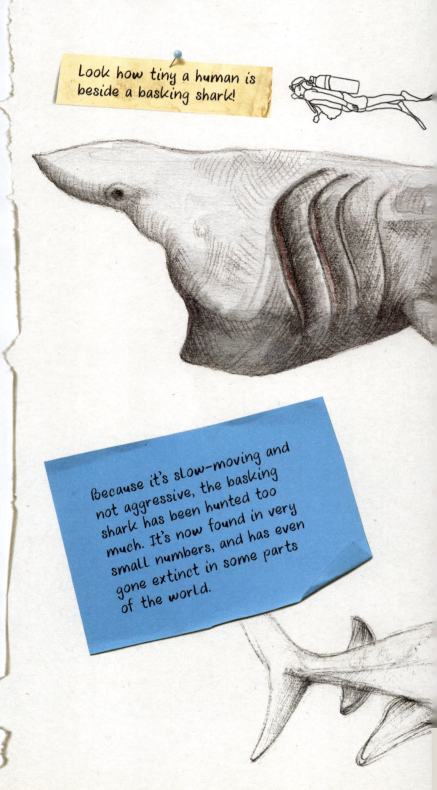

Look how tiny a human is beside a basking shark!

Because it's slow-moving and not aggressive, the basking shark has been hunted too much. It's now found in very small numbers, and has even gone extinct in some parts of the world.

The only fish on the planet bigger than the basking shark is the whale shark, which, believe it or not, also eats nothing but plankton.

Essential facts

↔ **SIZE:** At an average size of 5 to 7m, the basking shark is the second biggest fish in the world, and certainly the biggest fish in Irish waters. They can reach up to 12m in length, which means that they would be as tall as houses if they were able to stand up straight on their tails.

🏠 **HOME:** Basking sharks prefer cold water, which the seas around Ireland have a lot of. They are often seen in the area around the Blasket Islands in County Kerry.

🍴 **DIET:** Even though they have mouths that can open an entire metre wide, basking sharks only eat plankton.

🎂 **LIFE:** If all goes well, basking sharks can live for up to thirty-two years.

Glossary

algae
A kind of plant with no roots, leaves, or stem. Algae often grow in or near water.

amphibian
An animal that can live on land as well as in water, for example a frog or a newt.

BCE
Before the Common Era, meaning before the first century. Sometimes BC, meaning Before (the birth of) Christ is used instead.

carnivore
An animal that eats meat.

crustacean
An animal with a hard outer shell, for example a crab. Crustaceans usually live in water.

droppings
Solid waste (poo) produced by animals and birds.

echolocation
Some animals use sound to find their way around. They make a noise and then hear how the sound waves bounce off objects. This is called echolocation.

ecosystem
All the plants, animals, and other things that share a particular environment make up an ecosystem.

food chain
Bigger animals eat littler animals, who eat even littler animals – that is how the food chain works. So, for example, a shark is high up the food chain, and eats smaller fish which are lower down the food chain.

fur
The soft, thick hair that grows on some animals.

hedgerow
A row of bushes or shrubs, often at the edge of a road or field.

hibernate
Animals that hibernate spend the cold winter months sleeping.

invertebrate
An animal without a spine or backbone.

lowland pasture
Fields or grassy areas at a low level, not on high ground or the sides of mountains.

mammal
An animal that gives birth to live babies (instead of laying eggs, for example) and feeds its babies with milk from the mother's body. Mammals include cats, cows, and humans.

moult
To shed or lose some fur or hair, usually in the hotter summer months.

nectar
A sweet liquid produced by flowers, which is collected by bees and other insects. Honey bees use nectar to make their honey.

nutrition
The goodness that is in healthy foods.

plankton
Tiny plant and animal life found in the sea and eaten by some bigger fish and mammals.

predator
An animal that hunts and eats other animals.

reptile
An animal like a lizard that lays eggs, uses the heat of the sun to warm its body, and has hard or scaly skin.

rock pool (also known as tide pool)
A small pool of sea water surrounded by rocks.

rodent
A small animal with sharp front teeth. Rats, mice and squirrels are rodents.

rural
In or from the countryside, not the city – the opposite of urban.

scavenge
To search for food to eat, especially among rubbish.

sea level
Land that is not higher or lower than the height of the sea is at sea level.

tadpole
A baby frog or toad, after it hatches from frogspawn. Tadpoles have tails and no legs.

territory
The area of land that is controlled by a particular animal. If you have a pet cat, the area around your house is its territory; sometimes animals fight when one animal enters another's territory.

urban
In or from a town or city, not the countryside – the opposite of rural.

vegetation
Plants.

webbed feet
Feet that have skin stretching between the toes to help an animal swim are webbed.

wingspan
The distance from the tip of one wing to the tip of the other, measured when both wings are stretched open wide.

For my son David and the child I used to be. Aga

For my parents, who would always read to me inexhaustibly. Rob

Thank you to Nicola Marples, Professor in Zoology at Trinity College Dublin, for sharing her knowledge of the animals of Ireland and all her invaluable advice in the process of making this book.

The publisher also thanks editorial staff at Cois Life for their advice on Irish names for the animals.

DR HIBERNICA FINCH'S COMPELLING COMPENDIUM OF IRISH ANIMALS

First published in 2018 by
Little Island Books
7 Kenilworth Park
Dublin 6W
Ireland

Book concept by Aga Grandowicz & Rob Maguire

Illustrations, including cover images, and design © Aga Grandowicz 2018

Text © Rob Maguire 2018

The author and illustrator hereby assert their moral rights.
All rights reserved. No part of this book may be reproduced, transmitted or stored in a retrieval system in any form or by any means (including electronic/digital, mechanical, photocopying, scanning, recording or otherwise, by means now known or hereinafter invented) without prior permission in writing from the publisher.

ISBN: 978-1-910411-94-0

A British Library Cataloguing in Publication record for this book is available from the British Library.

Typeset by Aga Grandowicz
Printed in Poland by L&C Printing Group

Little Island receives financial assistance from The Arts Council/An Chomhairle Ealaíon and the Arts Council of Northern Ireland

Based in Dublin, Little Island Books has been publishing books for children and teenagers since 2010. It is Ireland's only English-language publisher that publishes exclusively for young people. Little Island specialises in publishing new Irish writers and illustrators, and also has a commitment to publishing books in translation.

As a child, Aga Grandowicz always wanted to be a vet or an ichthyologist, but she changed her mind before she started college and became an art director and a graphic designer instead. Originally from Gdynia in Poland, she's been living and working in Dublin since 2006. She is happiest when drawing furry animals and old trees or designing corporate identity.

Rob Maguire hails from the seaside town of Bray, Co.Wicklow, and has worked as a musician, a script supervisor, a journalist, a blogger and a bookseller. Now an advertising copywriter, Rob spends his time coming up with madcap ideas – such as writing a book about animals, despite being allergic to them.

10 9 8 7 6 5 4 3 2